Silly parrot
and other stories

Hannie Truijens

Illustrated by Annabel Spenceley

Silly parrot page 2

The hot air balloon page 10

Too many children page 18

Nelson

Silly parrot

Grandpa saw a lovely parrot
in the shop.
"I would like to buy this parrot,"
he said.
"But my wife
won't like it."
"I am sure she will," said the man
in the shop.

Grandpa took the parrot home.
It talked all day long.
"This silly parrot gives me a pain in the head," said Granny.
"Please take it away."

Grandpa took the parrot to Adam.
"Silly parrot, silly parrot,"
shouted the parrot.
"It's a clever parrot," said Helen.
"It makes too much mess," said Mum.
"Please take it away."

Adam took the parrot to school.
"Clever parrot, clever parrot,"
shouted the parrot.
"It's a funny parrot," said Jack.
"We can't keep a parrot at school,"
said Miss Black.
"Please take it home."

Jack took the parrot home.
"Funny parrot, funny parrot,"
shouted the parrot.
The parrot bit Liz.
"It's a bad parrot,"
said Jack's Mum.
"We don't want it here."

Jack took the parrot to Ali.
"Bad parrot, bad parrot,"
shouted the parrot, and
it pulled Sulima's hair.
"You nasty parrot," she said.
"Take the parrot away,"
said Ali's Dad.

Ali took the parrot to Colin.
"Nasty parrot, nasty parrot,"
shouted the parrot.
"I don't want a parrot in the
house," said Colin's Mum.
"But your Uncle will like it.
It's a lovely parrot."

Colin and Beth took the parrot
to their Uncle.
"Lovely parrot, lovely parrot,"
shouted the parrot.
"Yes, you are lovely,"
said Colin's Uncle.
"Will you come and live with me?"

The hot air balloon

"Would you like to fly
in my hot air balloon?"
asked Uncle Wilbur.
"Oh yes, we would,"
said Tom and Frank.
"Go and ask your Mum and Dad,"
said Uncle Wilbur.

Mum and the big boys helped Uncle Wilbur get the balloon ready.
"Why can't we come?" asked Helen and Adam.
"Sorry, but you are still too small," said Uncle Wilbur.

At last the balloon was ready.
Tom and Frank began to feel
a little scared.
"Going up is the easy part," said
Uncle Wilbur.
"It gets a little scary
when we go down."

As soon as they were up, the boys didn't feel so bad.
It was great fun to be way up in the sky.
"Look at our house down there," said Frank.
"It looks like a toy house."

Uncle Wilbur put more hot air
in the balloon and up they went.
The wind took the balloon away
from the houses.
Dad, Adam and Helen followed them
in the car.

They went over the river,
over the ponds, over the trees.
Uncle Wilbur sang.
Tom and Frank smiled
at each other.
They were very, very happy.

"Hold on boys, it's time to go down," said Uncle Wilbur.
The balloon went down and the houses and trees got bigger.
The car with Dad, Adam and Helen was close by.

The balloon came down
with a big bump.
Dad helped Uncle Wilbur and
the boys pack up the balloon.
"When will we be big enough?" asked
Adam and Helen.
"Soon," said Mum and Dad.

Too many children

Granny took Helen, Adam and all their friends to the sea.
"We will make a very big sandcastle," she said.

All the children helped Granny
to dig up sand.
They dug and dug, and
the sandcastle got bigger
and bigger.

"I am the king of the castle,"
said Adam.

"Give me back my ball," said Jack.

"Where are my shoes?" said Sulima.

"I want a drink," said Beth.

"I am the queen of the castle," said Liz.

"Help me, Granny," said Helen.

"My shoes are wet," said Ali.

"I want to eat," said Colin.

"Come on, children, let's eat,"
said Granny.
"I have buns and apples for you."
The water came up and went around
the sandcastle.

"It's time to go," said Granny.
"Helen broke my ball," said Ali.
"My shoes are full of sand,"
said Sulima.
"I want to sleep," said Beth.

"I had too many buns," said Adam.
"And I had too many apples," said Helen.
"And I had too many children," said Granny.